MW01463267

The Start of a Journey	2
Chapter 1: From the start	3
Chapter 2: A Life of Surrender	38
Chapter 3: Seeking the Face of God	57
Chapter 4: Relationship, not Religion	85
Chapter 5: Spread His Love	116
A word from the author	142

The Start of a Journey

"Direct me, Yahweh, throughout my journey so I can experience your plans for my life. Reveal the life-paths that are pleasing to you."

Psalms 25:4

Description

The Start of a Journey is about experiences we have along our journey with God. I pray that you grow in your relationship with God and experience all the possibilities that He has for you.

Chapter 1: From the start

EXPLANATION:
Over the years I have observed new believers start their journey and others who have been on their journey for some time, some with what seems like ease from the beginning, and others struggle and fall away, mainly because they feel that they have messed up too much because they don't see immediate change like others have and they don't

know where to look for help and because of this and a combination of other things. I want you to know that you're not alone in this struggle, this is the reason I felt led to write this book, to help others like me along the way. I will try to answer some questions throughout this book from my perspective to help assist you along your journey.

"Jesus continued, "In the same way, there will be a glorious celebration in heaven over the rescue of one lost sinner who repents, comes back home, and

returns to the fold—more so than for all the righteous people who never strayed away."
Luke 15:7 TPT

While I was starting to write some things down I asked God what He was saying to me and here I am following His leading not knowing that I was going to write this book, my prayer is that this book will help you in your journey whether you are just starting or if you are in a place of pause not knowing what comes next. God began showing me things that we go through at the start of our relationship with Him and I remembered that I spoke with my Lead Pastor from Byesville Ohio, Pastor Joe about starting a Sunday school class entitled "So I'm a Christian, now what" and after some discussion about the class content we landed on the name " New beginners Class" which was meant for people who had recently given their hearts to God and this class was to talk about what happens next.

It started when I felt God speaking to me about people starting a new life with Him and then falling away because they didn't know what to expect next or they would believe the lies of the devil that they didn't really accept Jesus in the first place because they didn't see immediate change where some people do and praise God for that, however, many people don't experience that immediately and feel like they must've done something wrong or it didn't really happen, and that was the reason and start of the class because every believer young and old in their faith alike need to know the start and what to expect next and receive encouragement from others in their situation and the Church Family, so we would talk about what it has been like so far in their new life with Jesus and the feelings we had along the way because it's very important that we discuss our feelings on the matter and get our questions answered by those who have been through similar experiences. For a little background on me when I first asked Jesus to be my Lord and Savior I did it because I thought it was what I was supposed to do, an obligation. After all, I grew up in a house of Christian believers, so naturally, I thought it was what I was supposed to do. There was no life change, there wasn't really any change at all and that was because I didn't mean it, I didn't ask Him because I wanted to but rather because my parents wanted me to, and ultimately the relationship with God would fail because it was just religion and going through the motions it wasn't real to me. There are also people who have received God in their life and it wasn't in the same way I did it and that maybe has ended up in religion as well and there are other situations and circumstances, this was my personal reason and experience so keep that in mind. I know that with being raised by a family of believers there are things that I might understand better or differently from the start however the same is true of those who weren't raised that way. Here are some questions that came up in our discussions.

 So why do I need Jesus? What is it that I need to be saved from? I mean things seem to be going just fine in my life, let's start with these questions which also happen to be some of the questions I had as well so let's start here. To understand these questions a little better we need to start at the beginning. First of all, we are born with a sinful nature because of the choices made by Adam and Eve which caused God to mercifully remove them from the Garden of Eden instead of ending their existence which many believed to be the case physically if they ate from the tree of the knowledge of good and evil.

"And the Lord God commanded the man, saying, "You may surely eat of every tree of the garden, but of the tree of the knowledge of good and evil you shall not eat, for in the day that you eat of it you shall surely die."
Genesis 2:16-17 ESV

So now the question is why could they not eat that fruit and why did they not die when they did? First, when they were created, it was to bring companionship to God, to walk with Him, to talk with Him which they did daily along with watching over and maintaining

God's creations. God had a specific plan in place to cultivate a relationship with His creation but also gave them free will to choose for themselves. He also created them with a desire to be with Him and gave man companionship with woman. The purpose of the Tree of the Knowledge of Good and Evil was not to tempt or deceive them, it was there to show that they had a choice. But yes when they ate from it they did in fact die, not physically but spiritually, when they did it caused a separation from God and made the sinful nature an option that wasn't noticed before because they were completely filled with Gods presence and glory. When they ate from that tree, that was the beginning of being separated from God's presence, and in doing so they had to be removed from the Garden of Eden where they were removed from a life continually in God's presence, thus a life separated from God began and the longer they were away from Gods presence the more their sinful natures became noticeable and the cost of their sin was now a real part of their lives. You see sin destroys our lives and it's not always visible or noticeable until it's too late. It's like being bound by a chain that you made link by link yourself until you are bound and unable to move. Just like in the Garden of Eden, the devil doesn't tell you the whole story, he provides enticing and desirable things to draw you into a false sense of safety and builds on your sinful desires until you are completely bound, yes you will be bound by your own desires. At that point you don't think you can ever get out or that there is any other option than giving up and continuing to go down a path of destruction with no hope of salvation or forgiveness, however, that's not the case.

 Throughout the Old Testament, we see the result of sin and the lengths people had to go to be forgiven they didn't have full access to be forgiven, they had to go to a priest with a sacrifice and the sacrifice had to be perfect no spots or blemishes no sickness or disease, and had to be the first fruits of their harvest.

"And on the seven days of the festival he shall provide as a burnt offering to the Lord seven young bulls and seven rams without blemish, on each of the seven days; and a male goat daily for a sin offering. And he shall provide as a grain offering an ephah for each bull, an ephah for each ram, and a hin of oil to each ephah. In the seventh month, on the fifteenth day of the month, and for the seven days of the feast, he shall make the same provision for sin offerings, burnt offerings, and grain offerings, and for the oil."
Ezekiel 45:23-25 ESV

As you can imagine that wasn't an easy find, beyond that God would only show Himself and speak to the prophets and a few chosen people at that time so you would have to seek them out if you wanted to hear from God or travel to a temple. That was the cost of sin separating us from God. That is what we needed saved from, an eternity without God and ultimately death itself. So why do we need Jesus? Well, Jesus is the spotless sacrifice that God offered for us to be able to come freely into His presence once again, Jesus is God's only son who walked on this earth fully God and fully man. Jesus endured going through everything that we go through, all the temptation all the choices to do right and wrong and He did it without falling into sin or giving into temptation, He lived a perfect life. We can read about this in **Matthew 4:1-11** When He was crucified on the cross He died for all of our sins so that we now had a way out, a way to be forgiven, and when He rose from the grave He had fully conquered death and became the only way into heaven. A new covenant began, we are to follow Jesus' example in how to live our lives.

As an example of what to do Jesus was baptized, the reason was to show how salvation operates in our life, showing others that we have surrendered our lives to God and are being washed clean, dying to our desires, being cleansed by the Spirit of God, and being raised into our new life in Jesus for all to witness.

"But when he waded into the water, John resisted him, saying, "Why are you doing this? I'm the one who needs to be baptized by you, and yet you come to be baptized by me?" Jesus replied, "It is only right to do all that God requires." Then John baptized Jesus. And as Jesus rose out of the water, the heavenly realm opened up over him and he saw the Holy Spirit descend out of the heavens and rest upon him in the form of a dove. Then suddenly the voice of the Father shouted from the sky, saying, "This is my

Son—the Beloved! My greatest delight is in him.""
Matthew 3:14-17 TPT

This is the beginning of a new life in Jesus and is hope for a life like you've never known before free from sin as we knew before.
"It's true that some of you once lived in those lifestyles, but now you have been purified from sin, made holy, and given a perfect standing before God—all because of the power of the name of the Lord Jesus, the Messiah, and through our union with the Spirit of our God."

1 Corinthians 6:11 TPT

So why do I need the Holy Spirit in my life? Isn't Jesus enough? Well yes, Jesus is enough but He is also part of the The Godhead God the Father, God the Son, and God The Holy Spirit. The Holy Spirit will empower us to live the way we need to, guiding us in the right direction and giving us boldness in times that we need it to witness to others.

"But when the Father sends the Spirit of Holiness, the One like me who sets you free, he will

teach you all things in my name. And he will inspire you to remember every word that I've told you."
John 14:26 TPT

The Holy Spirit is a very important part of your daily walk with God, not only does He help guide you He also helps you when you pray and He is The Spirit of God that dwells in us so we can have His presence with us as Adam and Eve did in the beginning.
 This walk and journey with God is full of learning new ways of

communicating, not only with God but with others and yourself, so continue growing with Him in every way possible. This should help with those questions from my perspective but I encourage you to seek God yourself and never stop.

The next thing or question I would like to talk about is repentance. What is repentance? I mean true repentance not just an I'm sorry I got caught mentality as my dad would say.

"You must prove your repentance by a changed life. And don't

presume you can get away with merely saying to yourselves, 'But we're Abraham's descendants!' For I tell you, God can awaken these stones to become sons of Abraham!"
Matthew 3:8-9 TPT

King David is one person who understood the importance of true repentance and being clean in the eyes of God, even though he lived before a time when Jesus died for our sins David was known as " A man after God's own heart". He made mistakes and failed again and again but he knew the importance of going before God and offering up all that he had and emptying every corner of his life in repentance to God, and by that I mean he would seek out God in such a way that he began to notice things in his life that haven't been turned over to God, he would then give them to God and truly repent and do everything that he could to never repeat what he had done.

Repentance itself is to turn away from your sin and to avoid doing it again, it's not being sorry because you got caught but it is a legitimate turning away, yes there will be times you might slip up but when you repent you do your best not to fall for it again. I know in my life when I'm tempted by something that I have previously fallen for I begin to recognize the tactics being used and when I have, it is easier to not fall for it the next time, now that being said the tactic will change if it no longer works but don't worry because when you read your Bible and pray consistently, The Holy Spirit will nudge you as a warning. True repentance is what purifies our spirit and covers us in The Blood of Jesus which is what God The Father sees when the day of judgment comes.

When sin is pointed out it's not just for judgment as you would think, it is a discipline and it is done out of love for growth, here is a good example from 2 Corinthians

"Even if my letter made you sorrowful, I don't regret sending it (even though I felt awful for a moment when I heard how it grieved you). Now I'm overjoyed —not because I made you sad, but because your grief led you to a deep repentance. You experienced godly sorrow, and as God intended, it brought about gain for you, not loss, so that no harm has been done by us. God designed us to feel remorse over sin to produce repentance that leads to victory. This leaves us with no regrets. But the sorrow of the world works death. Can't you see the good fruit that has come, as God intended, because of your remorse over sin? Now you are eager to do what is right! Look at the indignation you experienced over what happened and how alarmed you became.

What holy longing it awakened, what passion for God, and how ready you were to bring justice to the offender. Your response has proved that you are free of blame in this matter."
2 Corinthians 7:8-11 TPT

True repentance is meant to bring us closer to God and to help us live a life holy and acceptable before God as well as a good life for those around us, a good balance of forgiveness makes life a little more bearable if not for the other person it will for you.

"Let the words of my mouth and the meditation of my heart be acceptable in your sight, O Lord, my rock and my redeemer."
Psalm 19:14 ESV

"For we all have sinned and are in need of the glory of God."
Romans 3:23 TPT

You might say that you don't see anything wrong with what you are doing right now and to that I would say be careful, we are all in different places in our journey and God might not be dealing with you in certain areas of your life right now, and that is fine for where you are now, the time will come when it will need to be dealt with but if you are feeling that way in every area then I would encourage you to start asking God what it is that you need to do to draw closer to Him and what is it that you need to give to Him and not hold onto anymore.

"Mountain top experiences" (when things are going well) are great and are a well-needed rest but we don't live on the mountain top, we journey through valleys (hard times) as well.

"Even when your path takes me through the valley of deepest darkness, fear will never conquer me, for you already have! Your authority is my strength and my peace. The comfort of your love takes away my fear. I'll never be lonely, for you are near."
Psalms 23:4 TPT

Also, be careful when you feel that everything is going your way if you're not feeling battled for some time and you start to think that it's been a while then take an "internal inventory" as I call it because the devil doesn't fight what he's not threatened by and he won't get in the way of you doing your own thing, however when you start trying to do things Gods way he'll start fighting because he knows how powerful you are for the Kingdom of God and the impact that you will have. God's favor will put a target on your back, but it will take you higher than you ever thought possible. Remember that God promised that you would never be tempted above what you can handle and He will always provide a way out, so listen to the Spirits leading when you notice that you are struggling He will guide you.

"Be well balanced and always alert, because your enemy, the devil, roams around incessantly, like a roaring lion looking for its prey to devour."
1 Peter 5:8 TPT

"We all experience times of testing, which is normal for every human being. But God will be

faithful to you. He will screen and filter the severity, nature, and timing of every test or trial you face so that you can bear it. And each test is an opportunity to trust him more, for along with every trial God has provided for you a way of escape that will bring you out of it victoriously."
1 Corinthians 10:13 TPT

Chapter 2: A Life of Surrender

"Again I tell you, it is easier for a camel to go through the eye of a needle than for a rich person to enter the kingdom of God."
Matthew 19:24 ESV

There is a lot of misrepresentation surrounding this scripture, many believe that it is saying that you can't be rich and get into heaven, which of course is wrong. Jesus is talking about surrendering yourself fully and if you hold on to too much of your past and things that you have built up inside, you will be carrying too much baggage and struggle to live a life of surrender to God. "The eye of a needle" in those days was in reference to an entry to a city that was just large enough for people to travel through, however rich people would have camels with their wealth and baggage, the camel with all the things on its back was too large to pass through the gate or eye of the needle, so it would have to be capable of lowering itself and working its way through the gate, which was extremely difficult hence the reason for unloading the baggage and their wealth to get through that gate, whereas a "poor person" with no extra baggage would be able to pass through easier since they traveled with only what they could carry themselves. So as you can see it is a parable of surrender not of wealth. Allow God to carry your burden, your extra baggage, you don't need to do it alone, God will take what is weighing you down and replace it so that you might rest peacefully from it.

"Come to me, all who labor and are heavy laden, and I will give you rest. Take my yoke upon you, and learn from me, for I am gentle and lowly in heart, and you will find rest for your souls. For my yoke is easy, and my burden is light."
Matthew 11:28-30 ESV

When God got ahold of me and was drawing my heart to Him I could tell that it was different from anything I had ever experienced, I felt a deep connection in the core of my being that was never there before, and at that moment all I knew was that I needed Him in my life and nothing would get in my way of that. I was now saved but what did that mean? What was I supposed to do next? I knew the motions and the basics but now that I was serious I was adjusting to what I thought I knew. These were just a few of the questions that I needed answers to and I wasn't going to ask my parents or anyone in the church because what would they think of me? Would they think I faked the whole thing? Would they tell me that I should know

what came next or was there maybe something I did wrong for me not to know? I've learned we tend to carry everything alone and that isn't good because if you remember what I said earlier God created us for communication and with communication there is a bit of vulnerability mixed in, so we have to admit that we need help.
Think of it this way, when you get a job that you have zero experience at, it's the first, you obviously won't know what to do and you have to ask questions and you have to be "trained". You

tend to only talk to the trainer afraid of what the others might think and it might be something you should already know, but as time goes by you understand that it's ok to ask questions from anyone who works there and they're happy to help, so why are we so afraid to ask people in the church or leaders in the church. I know throughout history the church has seemed to lose sight of the vulnerability that we need to have, and in doing so it opens a door to "religion" and "self-righteous attitudes" that were never supposed to be. That being said use wisdom about what and how much you share with someone, they might not be in a place to receive that so have an accountability partner that can help you through these times. A lot of churches have small groups for many different types of classes. I pray that this book will help you along your journey ahead as a new believer or even someone who has struggled and happens to be stuck at the moment. So let's embark on this journey together.

I was thinking lately about my recent injury and how it seems that every time I get a break something seems to happen to slow my progress down and as I began to think about that I was reminded about everything that God has accomplished in and through my life.

There is a level of vulnerability that we all need to have that we have lost over generations of Christianity, people think that they have to be perfect and that is simply not the case, we all have failures and shortcomings that we experience nobody is exempt from that, nobody. The beginning is a hard and vulnerable time in a believers walk with God and we need to encourage each other and walk together, especially those who have been through it and have experienced firsthand the struggles of pretending to be "ok" so others didn't think less of them, that is a struggle that everyone, not just Christians experience, however, the church has seemingly made it more difficult for them because people think they have to meet a certain expectation or they won't be accepted and will be cast aside. I'm here to tell you that it is a lie from the pit of hell, we all have a starting point and where you are is exactly where God has met you, and your journey starts there, not at any other level. Just like they teach in sports you have to know the basics, the fundamentals are key to achieving success in that area. We look throughout life and we can see that it is true in every area, but for some reason, we have lost sight of that in our walk with Christ no matter the reason. Are you expected to stay where you start? Absolutely not, there is no excuse for staying in one place, it's called a journey for a reason, you might get stuck and stay in a place for a while but don't settle or get satisfied with that place we are to keep going.

"Isn't it obvious that all runners on the racetrack keep on running to win, but only one receives the victor's prize? Yet each one of you must run the race to be victorious. A true athlete will be disciplined in every respect, practicing constant self-control in order to win a laurel wreath that quickly withers. But we run our race to win a victor's crown that

will last forever. For that reason, I don't run just for exercise or box like one throwing aimless punches, but I train like a champion athlete. I subdue my body and get it under my control so that after preaching the good news to others I myself won't be disqualified."
1 Corinthians 9:24-27 TPT

There will also be times of resting, that are put there to help you gain strength for what is going to be the next season of your life.

"This is what the Lord says: "The people who survive the sword will find favor in the wilderness; I will come to give rest to Israel."
Jeremiah 31:2 NIV

Growing pains are real in your physical and spiritual body which means we will struggle at times and there will be times that can be painful, however, God is with you and will always prepare a way out but when you grow you will be sore, just like lifting weights you start with a comfortable weight to start for the level you are at and as you increase the weight and ability those growing pains and fatigue start but as you press through you begin to see the results of it all no matter how big or small. Your spiritual growth is the same way there will be struggles in areas where you were comfortable before that is the Holy Spirit letting you know it's time to grow in that area and move past your comfort zone. As you begin to exercise your faith and move towards a new goal you will start to experience growth which means there will be stretching which will cause levels of discomfort so be sure that you don't exceed what you're capable of doing at that moment, yes push yourself towards your goal to become more like Jesus but just like physical exercise if you do too much too fast there will be unnecessary pains and you will feel hurt and discouraged, so if that does happen don't focus on it and don't give up on yourself or your faith, it is a time to learn from what happened just like in life, you might know or you may not so keep praying and keep believing and the answer will be revealed. Many things will come your way but you have the strength to overcome them with the Holy Spirit so prayer and communication with God are very important not only at the beginning but throughout your walk, the more you communicate and read God's word which is the Bible the more you will grow to know what is in His heart for you and those around you and you will begin to surrender the parts of you that you couldn't before. As you grow in this life with God you will learn His voice and what needs to be surrendered to Him. I always told my boys and the teams that I had coached that practice doesn't make perfect and it never will, however, it will make your behaviors permanent and you will instinctively adjust when it's needed. We are constantly developing as people growing and developing, sometimes in ways we don't expect.

The reason for your continued growth is that somebody has been praying for help, for someone to understand them, and their circumstances and just be there for them, so remember that you are an answer to someone's prayer, you are the promise they have been waiting for. Never discount your value and importance on earth, you are fearfully and wonderfully made, and you have a purpose that only you can accomplish.

Chapter 3: Seeking the Face of God

"You will seek me and find me when you seek me with all your heart."
Jeremiah 29:13 NIV

As we learn to surrender our lives we have learned what it takes to seek the face of God. It's a daily walk but it doesn't mean that it's all that you do, rather surrender and seeking are tied into every part of your life and things like prayer and fasting become a

daily act of obedience without even thinking about it.
What is fasting? Generally, people associate fasting with going without food. Yes it can be however fasting goes beyond that, it is giving up something precious to you and giving that time to God, it might be food, it might be social media or video games, whatever it is, you are giving up your time with it and now that time has become Gods and you are spending it with Him. Praying, reading your Bible, worshipping, sitting in silence waiting to hear from God.

Whatever that time is, you gave up on what you wanted to do to spend time communicating with your creator and getting your next assignment.
The Bible says if you seek Him you will find Him.
So seek God with all your heart, mind, body, and spirit.
When you seek Him out, yes you will come across hardships trials, and temptations because the devil doesn't want you to get closer to God. After all, the moment you begin to get closer you start to realize who you are and what you are supposed to do

and that terrifies the devil and he will come against you in ways that you might not have expected. Why? Because he understands the moment you realize who you are in Christ Jesus he will have lost again. Don't misunderstand there will also be a lot of great times and experiences, we're just going over why the devil tempts and will try to deceive you so it's imperative that you read your Bible and pray, so you have a deeper understanding of who God is and you will also understand His voice like never before. So why doesn't the devil just leave you alone, well when you're not doing things for God then he doesn't need to do anything really because he has you and your thoughts so the devil will give you things you want to keep you from looking to God because you are living your best life or so you may believe. So the reason the devil fights you and tempts you is that he understands who you are meant to be and you don't fight what you're not threatened by, thieves don't break into empty homes so now the question shouldn't be why is the enemy fighting me, but rather what does the enemy know about you that you don't know about yourself, why is the devil so threatened by who you will become and I've said it before, there is a job to be done that only you can do there are people who need Jesus that only you can reach and others who are waiting for you to share your story with them about all the things that God has done in your life and how that no matter what God has never left you or abandoned you and has given you peace that doesn't make sense because you are a child of The Most High, you are sons and daughters of God so keep fighting to keep seeking His face and see how far you can go. The gift of salvation is free to all who will accept it but the journey will cost you and it is worth it. I'm reminded of what David said in 1 Chronicles 21:24 where he was looking for a place to build an alter to God so that the plague would stop and he told the owner that he wanted to pay full price to which the owner said that he couldn't accept and that he would even provide a bull for the sacrifice saying take it! Do whatever you like and David said that he would not take for the Lord what belonged to someone else nor would he give an offering that cost him nothing. So as you go through these trials remember that you are learning from them not only how to just get through them but how to put your trust in The Lord, your sacrifices do cost you but they also allow you to seek God out and begin a life seeking the face of God and don't lessen your experience by thinking that your not worth it or you don't know where to start. Seeking God is always worth it. I can honestly say that you won't be disappointed if you do so, and when you do you might not expect how you find Him, it may be in a vision or dream, or it might be in the person that you have been praying for but you will see Him. I have seen Him in different ways and places some I would've expected and others I wouldn't have, I have seen Jesus in visions and dreams as well through the lives of people I have prayed for and those I never knew He also shows Himself in our thoughts and other times just a single word that you might overhear so never limit God to your expectations or experiences. Getting to know God is a journey in itself but as you get to know Him more you will begin to see, hear, and think differently than you have before. Let me explain, God is Love and as you grow closer to Him the more you will begin to Love differently than you might have known because you begin to see yourself and others how God sees them and there will be times when you don't understand why you are feeling that way towards someone you don't know, it does not love the way the world loves but rather it is a perfect Love that confounds even the brightest scholar yet it's simple and compassionate. Some will call it unconditional love and though that is true it goes even deeper than that. God is Love

"Then, by constantly using your faith, the life of Christ will be released deep inside you, and the resting place of his love will become the very source and root of your life. Then you will be

empowered to discover what every holy one experiences—the great magnitude of the astonishing love of Christ in all its dimensions. How deeply intimate and far-reaching is his love! How enduring and inclusive it is! Endless love beyond measurement that transcends our understanding—this extravagant love pours into you until you are filled to overflowing with the fullness of God!"
Ephesians 3:17-19 TPT

I also love how the NIV says it in verse 19

"and to know this love that surpasses knowledge that you may be filled to the measure of all the fullness of God"
To know God is to know Love itself. I know that the closer I get to The Father the more I know His heart and the more I love those around me. Don't get me wrong I'm nowhere near perfect nor have I "mastered" God's love, I'm merely a servant of The Lord trying to do what I can to be more like Jesus, and like most of you there are times when I see glimpses of His Love in my life and my spirit longs for those

times, I know because I can feel it, I feel it in the same way I knew without knowing that I saw Jesus in a dream that I had. Let me share that with you.

I was carrying people across a great body of water to Him and as I walked the water parted at each step, and as I got closer He opened His arms and would take the people who were injured and said that He would make them whole again. I remember that feeling so completely and I'll never forget it, in that moment I felt such love, power, compassion, and Holy judgment all at the same time. They were so pure and unaltered in any way I have never felt anything like it in my life. When I woke up I immediately set up thinking did I really just see Jesus? I could barely breathe and all of a sudden I knew that it was true as my spirit began to cry out to Him as I had never experienced before as it was trying to leave my body just to be with him and I could tell that my spirit was crying out with everything it had because the feeling of longing that I had, I couldn't stop crying to the point that I woke up my wife as I was gripping my chest with such sorrow that I had seen the face of the one who gave His very life for me. Now that is the only time I have ever felt that way, it was familiar yet a mystery. The closest feeling that I could think of at that moment was of deep mourning for the loss of the closest person in your life and yet that feeling of longing to be with my Lord and Savior was even stronger than that but at the same time, I felt a deep love that changed my life from that day on. Until then I couldn't understand truly what it was to love so deeply, so completely and so unconditionally that it hurt physically.

 I have experienced loss as I know many of you have as well and yes even though it hurts this was different and by no means am I pushing away your feelings for those loved ones, I am just trying to explain in my limited understanding how it felt in the deepest part of me that I never knew existed.

When we seek the Face of God we will see things in a different light and what we thought we knew begins to change, our thoughts and desires take a new focus as we begin to see as God sees.

God Loves you and He is actively seeking you, He hasn't forgotten about you nor has He overlooked you at any time in your life. You might have a thought or a dream/vision or you might just feel happy and at peace about something, you never know how He will show up in your life but He is there. Another question I've had asked has been why are there so many denominations if there's only one God. As you might have figured out through your own life so far we as people interpret things differently we see things differently, so as you can tell many people strive to serve God in the way that someone has interpreted that process. Now before I say anything else I want you to understand that you need to seek the face of God and whichever denomination you choose to attend make sure that they preach God's Word and that it is a place where you can grow and draw closer to God spiritually and if you can't, find a church that does. It is absolutely vital that you can grow in your journey with God and that every day you seek Him becoming more like Jesus. So you must be part of a church that follows and preaches The Bible and study it for yourself don't rely only on others to feed you so that you can grow, start reading The Word of God and feed yourself as well, that way you will know if something is right or wrong. We need to know how to seek God and how to listen to Him so that we know what to do based on what He says and go where He leads. So learn to listen to His still small voice so that you won't be deceived by others.

Remember the bigger the plan or calling God has for you, the greater the testing because God can't put you in a place of power or influence if you haven't been tested or taught how to handle yourself when times of great pressure come, you need to be ready, things will happen that test you and push you, and you need to be confident that through any situation you know how to give it to God, lean on His wisdom and hold firm in times of great difficulty. Think about diamonds they are strong, and beautiful and are made under immense pressure, so what starts as carbon is put through extreme temperatures and pressure to become one of the strongest materials on earth, carbon is also essentially what makes graphite (pencil lead) so trust the process, God has a plan written just for you! Trust in God, let Him lead you, and talk daily with Him and you will know what to do when the pressure starts.

"Though we experience every kind of pressure, we're not crushed. At times we don't know

what to do, but quitting is not an option."
2 Corinthians 4:8 TPT

Never give up on what God has placed in your heart, even when you're feeling crushed or defeated, remember that you are not, just hold on victory is closer than you think. All this requires faith, so what is faith? Faith is more than just believing something is going to happen when there's no evidence of it happening, however, that is a good place to start. Faith recognizes that we need God because we can't do it.

"He told them, "It was because of your lack of faith. I promise you, if you have faith inside of you no bigger than the size of a small mustard seed, you can say to this mountain, 'Move away from here and go over there,' and you will see it move! There is nothing you couldn't do!"
Matthew 17:20 TPT

We act in accordance with faith and obedience to The Father when we feel a calling in a certain area of our life or if it's an area that we are called to work in for ministry, remember who God calls He equips and the question isn't are you called but where. That is a discussion between you and God so walk obediently where He calls you, that doesn't mean it's pastor, evangelist, or missionary, it could be helping out setting things up at church or an event or it could be in your household which all of us are called to serve in since being a husband, wife, father, and mother are the biggest impact not only to your immediate family but to those who are watching you. It could be your workplace, you see the closeness here these are all relational in nature God wants a relationship with you in all areas of our lives. Pray for God's will in all things and ask what He'll have you do every day, ask for a chance to bless someone even through a smile or a single word to bring joy or revelation into their lives. Jesus gave us an example of how to pray in Matthew 6:9-13. Now like I said before prayer is just simply talking to God, but what we have here is a layout that we can follow, what I mean is we want the will of God in our lives here on earth just as it is in heaven, we want God to give us sustenance for our day so that we can be filled with His Holy Spirit so that we can speak into the lives of others, we also want forgiveness not just for our sins but also for what we have done wrong against someone else, we also need to forgive those who have done us wrong and we need His wisdom and His help to avoid temptations that come against us every day as well as a way out of what we are struggling with at that moment. So as you can see this prayer is an outline of things that we should be praying for in our prayer time.

Chapter 4: Relationship, not Religion

"God, listen to my prayer! Don't hide your heart from me when I cry out to you!"
Psalms 55:1 TPT

Since the beginning God intended to have a relationship with us, to walk with us and talk with us. This is at the core of our relationship with God and is also the core of any relationship that is to be successful and last, this isn't a coincidence. Just as that is true so it is that our relationship with God needs to be at the top and take priority. To have a successful relationship you need to communicate with the other person, notice I said "with" and not "to". This is very important because we both need to be heard and we both need to speak for the relationship to last. This is one of the most basic parts of a relationship, and to communicate with God is to talk with Him (Prayer) and read His word (The Bible) this will begin to allow you to hear what He has to say through His Word and your life, you'll notice that when God speaks to us, it happens in many ways and I'm not going to limit how He will speak to you but here are some examples. God could speak audibly, through your thoughts, through a memory (like He did with parts of this book to me), through what someone else says (you'll know), through something that you see, smell, or hear. As you can see there are many ways that God will speak to you so we need to listen, and to do that we need to grow closer in our communication with Him through prayer and reading The Bible so we begin to understand His heart. He will not always speak in the most flashy or expected ways as Elijah found out here in 1 Kings

"The Lord said, "Go out and stand on the mountain in the presence of the Lord, for the Lord is about to pass by." Then a great and powerful wind tore the mountains apart and shattered the rocks before the Lord, but the Lord was not in the wind. After the wind, there was an earthquake, but the Lord was not

in the earthquake. After the earthquake came a fire, but the Lord was not in the fire. And after the fire came a gentle whisper. When Elijah heard it, he pulled his cloak over his face and went out and stood at the mouth of the cave. Then a voice said to him, "What are you doing here, Elijah?""
1 Kings 19:11-13 NIV

I love it when The Holy Spirit speaks to us. One example that I can think of is the time I was walking alone one day nothing out of the ordinary I was single at the time, however, I was wondering if anyone was thinking about me or if they even cared, I was just having one of those days, anyway as I was walking I heard in a small whisper "Happy Birthday" and I started to cry because I didn't even remember that it was my birthday, I know it might seem like a small thing to some people but in that moment it meant everything to me, knowing that even though I thought I wasn't worth remembering God knew what to say to me in that moment, no it wasn't a heavy revelation or world-changing but it was a simple communication with me and the warmth and love that I felt changed how I felt that day. Through your talks with God remember that you don't have to put up some lengthy, wordy prayer it can simply be a normal conversation like any other. Tell Him how you're feeling and what's going on because He cares and He listens, but also take time to wait and listen. There isn't always time to wait in a moment but there are always times that we can. I love the way

The Passion Translation says it, these are some strong words.

"Here's what I've learned through it all: Don't give up; don't be impatient; be entwined as one with the Lord. Be brave and courageous, and never lose hope. Yes, keep on waiting—for he will never disappoint you!"
Psalms 27:14 TPT

I know that I have talked a lot about The Holy Spirit speaking and I understand that some might not be aware that The Holy Spirit is an active part of The

Godhead as well as an active part in your life. In The New Testament Jesus talks about sending a helper, an advocate, or a Divine encourager depending on the translation.

"And I will send you the Divine Encourager from the very presence of my Father. He will come to you, the Spirit of Truth, emanating from the Father, and he will speak to you about me." **John 15:2, 26 TPT**

He is talking about The Holy Spirit, He came to give us

strength and courage to complete what God has for us to do. He also comforts us in time of need and when you don't know what to say He will help you find the words of your heart. As an example, there was a time in my relationship with my wife that we didn't communicate very well and there were things we said or did that made each other mad and it was even affecting the children, we never thought anything about it other than how we felt in those moments and it began tearing the family apart. I would pray asking God what we were doing wrong something had to change in our relationship or we might not last. One day as I was praying asking God for help and The Holy Spirit asked what are you doing now? I replied "I don't understand" so He replied what is it that we are doing right now? So I replied we are talking. That seemed to be the end of the conversation and I was left wondering what it meant. Later I had an idea to sit down at the end of the day with the whole family and talk about our day, I wasn't sure if that would even help our situation and doing it would feel uncomfortable since it was something that was so out of the ordinary for us and as I expected it was an awkward few days, then it started getting easier to talk with each other, then about a week or two later as I was praying I felt we needed to go deeper in our conversations, but how? I mean we are all talking and that's more than we did before. While in prayer I felt The Holy Spirit ask "Are you satisfied?" and to be honest I wasn't, because even though we were talking we were still feeling upset with each other, and not much had changed. So as I thought about what we needed to do, I had another idea, now let me be clear it had to be God because frankly, I'm not that smart so in this instance He gave me wisdom. That night when we sat down to talk we started with prayer as usual and I said we were going to start something different, something that we'd never done before and though it seemed unusual and different we would go around the table, and one at a time would say what aggravated us that day that someone at the table did, this was, of course, an unusual idea since nobody wants to say anything that will cause a problem so I said when we do there will be no retaliation or comments from the person not talking and when it's our turn we are not to talk about what that person said in a bad way because these are feelings that are real and we need to let them out. I instructed everyone to start with me or if they felt comfortable just talk to whoever it might be. As you can imagine that was a quiet night so we read the Bible together, prayed then went to bed. As the days went by we began to slowly trust that we were going to be heard and we began talking about what made us feel negatively towards the other person and how it affected us. After a few months, we became so comfortable that we didn't wait for our sit-down family time and would tell the other person that we were hurt or frustrated by what was just said in that moment and we didn't argue, we apologized sincerely, and went about our day and when we'd sit down at night we had less and less to say that was negative and we began talking about what made us happy that day, what we were thankful for and what we could do moving forward. I have to say that during that time and moving forward I loved my family more and felt closer than ever before now don't get me wrong I loved my family dearly, however, I felt a closeness like never before and we all grew closer from this.

Now I know this might not work for everyone but it's what I felt we needed to do and I tell you that story to show how important communication is in a relationship whether it's with other people or with God The Father, communication is vital for any relationship. Just like any relationship it is not a game and yes you can fall away or "backslide" is the Christian term or as The Passion Translation says "drifting off course". We need to be careful that we don't drift away from The Love of God because when we do we are opened up to something entirely different. Things might feel good for a time but understand that you are only imprisoning yourself in a cell that is slowly closing and when time is up and Jesus returns for His bride (The Church) then that prison that you put yourself in will close and you'll be lost forever. We will only enter Heaven if we have a relationship with Jesus, He was the sacrificial Lamb, the Son of God, and the only one who has never sinned. Jesus is both God and man. That's why He was born of a virgin because if He wasn't He would've been born into a sinful nature like the rest of us. Our relationship with Jesus is the only way that the sin we've had forgiven is hidden, it's covered by the Blood of The Spotless Lamb of God. Through Jesus, and Him alone our sins have been forgiven and I'm so glad that I don't have to live this life out wondering if I could ever be forgiven for what I've done in my life.

"This is why it is so crucial that we be all the more engaged and attentive to the truths that we have heard so that we do not drift off course."
Hebrews 2:1 TPT

So if communication is so important then Why does Jesus speak in parables? Parables are stories with both moral and spiritual meanings. I understand that sometimes it's hard to know what is being said. Sometimes it's to speak to certain individuals, sometimes it's to have you seek the answer out because what He says has specific interpretations for specific times with the same parable. Now Jesus also speaks clearly and that is to be listened to and sought out just the same, the difference is the importance and accountability in the moment. Let me explain, the more clearly the Holy Spirit speaks to you whether in dream, vision, or in your quiet time. The more accountable you are for what you've heard if it was a specific instruction, not a parable to be interpreted in time or at your leisure, there is typically a deadline for it to be accomplished. Therefore it is crucial that you follow the instructions to the letter and in the time that you were given the revelation. Not all things are to be done immediately some happen over years of development however both are important so if the instruction is not fully clear then seek the answer through prayer and reading His Word, I have found that the more I read The Bible the more I understand and the more I realize how God speaks to us. There are many times that I've read something and each time I have read it I have found more insight and wisdom of what's been said. I understand that many are very cautious of what they do or say so the big question is, what happens if you make a mistake? Well simply put you made a mistake that's it you're human. If you make a mistake in what you heard that's ok it happens don't stay in that mindset because you were listening to what God had to say and you might've misinterpreted it because you put too much of yourself into it, a lot of times I've heard from God I have said "Father, that is impossible! I don't have the capability or knowledge to even start …..", rest assured that if God has called you to something then He will provide everything that you need to complete it, you just have to step out in faith even if you can't see that next step. Also, understand that not everybody is ready to hear what is being said and started yet. So seek God to know if what is being said is ready to be talked about and to whom. There were things that Jesus shared with His disciples but not others until later and other times like in Luke 8:9-10 he discusses that he will speak deeper about the parable that was just spoken because the disciples had a teachable heart to perceive the secret hidden mysteries of God. That was because they have spent time with Him daily. Now yes, Jesus is both God and man and though he walked this life the same as we do he did not sin. Jesus Loves us so much that He chose to go through this life so that He could have a better relationship with us and go through the same things that we have been through.

"Then Jesus was led up by the Spirit into the wilderness to be tempted by the devil."
Matthew 4:1 ESV

While Jesus was in the wilderness, He was tempted by different things the same as we are. Now understand the temptations are the same yet delivered in different ways because what works on me might not work on you and the same way as what may tempt a man might not tempt a woman. But the categories would be the same. I say this to point out that The devil hasn't changed in all these years and he also knows the Bible front to back. He has lived through it all and has been twisting the Word of God to create confusion and division amongst the people of this world since his fall. That is one reason we have so many arguing about what the Bible means. Even though there is confusion surrounding the Word of God, when we read it and when we listen to the Holy Spirit we begin to have a better understanding of what God is saying and we are able to combat the arguments with Love and understanding, that however doesn't mean that we need to seek out the confrontation, trust me it will find you but like the Bible says, study to show yourself approved. This is how we communicate with God, reading His Word and prayer. The more we do the easier it is to know right from wrong and truth from lies. The Bible also says that some things will take more than prayer alone and that is only accomplished through prayer and fasting. What that means is that you are setting aside something important to you, in many cases that is food, but it is important to understand what God wants you to *fast.* While you're praying ask Him what you are to give up and for how long. During this time you will begin to draw even closer to God and you will see a way out of what you are going through. I have been through a good amount of things throughout my life and in no way am I minimizing what others have gone through because many have been through a lot more, but each one of us has been through these experiences. Some things we have been victorious over and others we are struggling through even now. It's not what you go through but how you go through it. We need to understand that we are not alone, no matter how much it feels like we are. Some have friends and family, others may not. However, God is always with us through everything that we go through but are we willing to say "God I trust you" and mean it? He will always be there when we feel our lowest and we somehow know that everything will be ok. That is the relationship that we have with Him and it goes far beyond that. The most important thing is to know that you are not alone, ever. God sent His only Son to this earth to walk with us and teach us how to live, when He conquered death, hell, and the grave, He opened the way for the Holy Spirit to be with us. You are never alone, I can't express that enough. Knowing how many times throughout my life that I have felt alone I must tell you there is hope there is a way for you to stand victorious at the end of what seems like an eternal suffering.

Chapter 5: Spread His Love

"Then you will be empowered to discover what every holy one experiences—the great magnitude of the astonishing love of Christ in all its dimensions. How deeply intimate and far-reaching is his love! How enduring and inclusive it is! Endless love beyond measurement that transcends our understanding—this extravagant love pours into you until you are

filled to overflowing with the fullness of God!"
Ephesians 3:18-19

Your journey is not going to be immediate, it will take time and the same goes for those whom you share your faith and journey with. The Bible tells us about types of ground that we will come across as we spread His word it is found in Luke 8:4-15 where Jesus speaks to a crowd of people and gives a parable which I mentioned before is a story where there are both moral and spiritual truths and meanings.

This parable talks about farmers sowing seeds and how they would typically sow the seeds was throwing them across the ground and in doing so the seeds would fall on good and bad types of ground leading to difficulties depending on where they landed, some would land on a pathway and as a result the seeds were trampled and ultimately become seeds for the birds to eat, another place mentioned was on a rocky path where the seeds were able to sprout but not able to take root for continued growth from lack of moisture. Another type of ground was covered in weeds and the seeds were unable to grow to full maturity because all the weeds surrounding them wouldn't allow their growth. Let me explain some of these types of "problem grounds" so we can look deeper into this parable.

Landing on the hard pathway to be trampled and become seed for birds ultimately allows others to be fed by the same seed that was meant to be planted is bringing life to those not originally intended but still have a purpose greater than we realize, you never know who is watching or listening when you talk witness to others. The next is landing on the gravel, it relates to how some of us came to know Jesus, we wanted to know Him, however, we weren't in the best place for growth and withered over time whether it be our own disinterest or our situation, however, don't be discouraged because we can reconnect to the Living Water source which is Jesus and no matter the ground he can move in our lives and plant us where we can thrive in Him. The last "problem ground" is the ground covered in weeds and that would be an example of coming to Jesus and none of your friends, family, or coworkers understand what you have discovered and won't allow you to talk about your faith and they criticize you for it and ultimately choke out your faith. However, don't be discouraged and continue to seek the face of God in those seemingly impossible circumstances and be the example to them that God has placed you there for because that is your mission field for the time being and even if it's not with words let God shine through your words and deeds let them see the fruit that is being produced by your faith because they are watching even though they won't tell you.

You see there are many parts to sharing the Love of God with others, you can be the one to plant seeds, water them, care for them, or harvest. All of these are crucial and of the utmost importance for where the individual is in that moment of their life. Sometimes you plant and you're the person to tell them about Jesus, sometimes you water or care for the seed, being there to encourage and pray for and continue to witness through your words and actions, at other times you witness the harvest being the one to in some cases bring that person to God so they can start their journey with guidance and love. There are also times when you will be the one who does it all but don't be discouraged if you "just plant the seed" because without that seed being planted no matter the ground it falls on there will never be a harvest, so please don't stop when you don't see the harvest, God called us to spread the gospel not just harvest after all the work is done. Every part of this process is important and the whole process brings us back to the relationship because God wants a personal relationship with you, The God of all creation wants to walk and talk with you daily, a friend who sticks closer than any other is how He is described in Proverbs 18:24 Remember there is something that needs to be done that only you can do and somebody is waiting for you. Understand that you are the promise for somebody's life and they are waiting for that encounter. Share your experience and your testimony with passion and without regret or fear with others who are becoming new believers and starting a new relationship with God. It is up to us to share what we have learned throughout the years and to cultivate growth for relationships and not just religion, there are enough religions out there and we need the world to know that time is running out and that Christianity itself needs to be a relationship with God as it was intended from the beginning. We're not here to beat Jesus into anyone but to deliver a truth with love and compassion. There are so many people who have been shown religion and left to their own devices and not shown how to cultivate a relationship with God and move beyond what they have seen as religious people with tons of rules, yes there are things to which we abide and as you grow closer to God the more you want to be like Jesus and the example He gave which in turn changes the old you to who you are meant to be. We don't walk this journey alone, we all have to be there for each other to help uplift, encourage, and pray to name just a few things, so doesn't it make sense to just be there for someone who is starting out and not sure which step to take next? Be there for each other, encouraging one another to live life as the best version of yourself and the person God called you to be showing the Love of God. If you're not sure the best way to move forward then I would suggest connecting with your church and helping when you have the opportunity to do so and through this act of service you can learn what needs to be done while helping others along the way. I would also encourage you to witness and show kindness whenever the opportunity presents itself. Remember there was a time when you didn't realize that you were doing something wrong so be patient when speaking to others and never talk down to anyone. Remember when you do a certain behavior for a long time you don't think that it's wrong so you continue doing that behavior until you see an example of what you are supposed to be doing or that what you have been doing is hurting you and those around you and at that time you no longer want to do that behavior, that isn't always easy as you well know, however that is what growth in Jesus is like, you come to him just as you are and as you begin to grow closer to him through prayer and reading The Bible you will start to feel that some things that you are doing are not right and that you need to change, that is called "conviction" and when you feel convicted about something it's because you now know that it is wrong and a lot of times this is where people think that it's all about rules but that's not the case, but for so long religious people have been shaking their fingers at people for what they are doing and ignoring what they themselves are doing is wrong and are called hypocrites because they go around like they are perfect and do nothing wrong but deep inside they are hurting and struggling just like we all do. That keeps people out of church and away from "religion" That is what kept my dad away from knowing Jesus for so long, he would say that he remembered the church people would act like nothing was wrong on Sundays and then see the same people walking into bars or staggering out of them and in his mind he was a better person than they were. Now we don't know where anyone is in their own journey and walk with God and I'm in no way judging what was done but as Christians, we are being watched to see if what we "preach" is real. People are lost and they are looking for truth. Remember before when I said that after my dream my spirit was trying to get back to Jesus because it was longing to be with Him? That's what is going on deep inside them and their spirits are longing for Jesus and to be with Him. Like I always told my children "Don't judge others just because they have sinned differently than you". This is so true because sin is sin there are no different levels even though some things are worse than others that's not for us to judge. God is a great God and is Love but He is also a Just God and when the day comes that we are to stand before Him we will be judged and on that day we will have to answer for what we've done and what we didn't do that we could've done. The only saving grace is Jesus and if we know Him and have a relationship with Him that is the only way that all of our sins will be washed by the blood that He spilled on that cross when He became The perfect Sacrifice and the only one who could've done it. Because of Jesus, we have the opportunity to live life and have a personal relationship with Him, and live with our first love, our creator, and our Savior forever. My prayer is that you will understand this relationship with God more than you did or that it reminds you of what you need to do to help those who are struggling or have just received Jesus as their Savior and help them wherever they are in their journey. Everyone needs help along the way, you might have just asked Jesus to be Lord of your life or have known Him personally already and are not sure what to do. You might also still be looking to see if you would even be capable of God's grace and mercy and if that's the case rest assured that yes, you are loved by God and He is waiting for you to reach out to Him.

A person who is hungry for God will seek His Face every day, not only on Sundays. When we seek the face of God daily and we are "Hungry" for Him then we see the world as He sees it and we become more passionate and loving but we also become more attentive to our surroundings and know more about the schemes of the devil and are more prepared for whatever comes our way, no we won't catch everything and that happens, however, we will know how to overcome what takes us by surprise.

"We all experience times of testing, which is normal for every human being. But God will be faithful to you. He will screen and filter the severity, nature, and timing of every test or trial you face so that you can bear it. And each test is an opportunity to trust him more, for along with every trial God has provided for you a way of escape that will bring you out of it victoriously."
1 Corinthians 10:13 TPT

We need to take what we have learned throughout our journey and share it with others who are starting theirs or those who are struggling. We must reach out to those who are reaching out to us for help. We are to share the wisdom and experience with others to encourage them and ourselves because when you share your story it encourages us and reminds us of all God has done for us, that is called your testimony and that is the experience that no one can ever take away from you because you lived through it, you overcame it by the grace of God and now you have a story to tell. So ask God to show you what you are to do each day and ask Him to place someone in your path so that His Love in your life can make a difference in there's.

*"For every spiritual infant who lives on milk is not yet pierced by the revelation of righteousness. But solid food is for the mature, whose spiritual senses perceive heavenly matters. And they have been adequately trained by what they've experienced to emerge

with an understanding of the difference between what is truly excellent and what is evil and harmful."
Hebrews 5:13-14 TPT

Your story can be one of victory or defeat so walk your journey well and make it a victorious one.
  -Larry Nicola

I'll leave you with this message we find here in **Matthew 28:18-20** often referred to as "The Great Commission" where Jesus tells us to go into the world wherever we may go spread his word and make disciples. This is what we are meant to do along our journey in Him so as you spread the word of God and share what He has done for you along your journey train others to follow Jesus and to seek His face and follow His example the best we can, may God bless you as you carry out His will in your life and to bring as many as we can to His glorious kingdom because time is short the signs are there and scripture is being fulfilled in front of our eyes so be ready.

The scriptures used are TPT "The Passion Translation". I love reading in different translations however The Passion Translation seems to be worded for easier reading.

A word from the author

The one thing I enjoy about writing is the fact that God continues to open up His Word to me and teach me new things as I read and listen to Him. I've truly been thankful for the opportunity to write, honestly, I never expected to nor did I have any desire to, however, God opened my eyes to something new to help reach others in a way that I would never have been able to before. So be open to the possibilities of what God will do

through you and when the opportunity arises know that you have been prepared and through everything that you have been through you have grown and that all those growing pains that you go through are preparing you for something that only you can do You are one of a kind and Loved by the One who is Love itself and the creator of everything. I pray for each of you daily not only for your journey but for your growth and development of who you are becoming.
I encourage you to share this book when you are finished with

it especially if you feel led to give it away to someone or whatever God lays on your heart.
Encourage those around you to go deeper than ever before and support each other's journey.

"If you will teach the believers these things, you will be known as a faithful and good minister of Jesus, the Anointed One. Nurture others in the living words of faith and in the knowledge of grace which you were taught."
1 Timothy 4:6 TPT

Made in the USA
Columbia, SC
08 October 2024

996a3743-54f7-44d2-8d5b-fb9e0ae47bffR01